ZION MOUNTAIN RANCH

Copyright © 2023 Kelsey Reynolds. Illustration copyright © 2023 Kelsey Reynolds. Font copyright © 2019 Wellscript Studio. All rights reserved. No part of this book may be reproduced or transmitted in any form or by any means, electronic or mechanical, including photocopying, recording, or by any information storage and retrieval system, without written permission from the author.
Neither the author or publisher assumes any responsibility or liability whatsoever on behalf of the consumer or reader of this material. Any perceived slight of any individual or organization is purely unintentional.
Neither the author or publisher can be held responsible for the use of the information provided within this book.
I have made every effort to contact all copyright holders.

For information address kbreynolds.rn@gmail.com.

First hardcover edition: July 2023.

Paperback ISBN: 979-8-9882463-2-9
Hardcover ISBN: 979-8-9882463-3-6
Ebook ISBN: 979-8-9882463-4-3

Illustrations attributed to Midjourney AI and Zion Mountain Ranch.

Printed by IngramSpark in the USA.

BadgerBooks, LLC
Salt Lake City, UT
www.badgerbooks.org

Dedicated to Todd, Erika, Oliver, & Claire

Preface:

Experience a truly authentic western destination nestled in the breathtaking mountains of Zion National Park. Not only does it offer premier lodging options, but it is also home to a remarkable roaming herd of buffalo. Discover this unique haven now at www.ZMR.com for an unforgettable experience of a lifetime.

Morning sun rises
Red rocks, canyons, nature's maze
Mountains beckon, explore

Majestic bison
Harmoniously roaming
Fields of solitude

Amidst rustic charm
Cordwood's pancakes and berries
Family laughter

Great Pyrenees roam

Guardians of sacred grounds

Slumbering in peace

Miniature horses
Munching hay from open hands
Nuzzles crave more treats

Mother hen and chicks
Chirping a musical song
Free range on pasture

Peanut and Popcorn
Slimy noses squeal and snort
Rolling in the dirt

Rhythmic hooves gallop
Echoing tranquil canyons
Western adventure

Running water calms
Sustainable growth blossoms
Greenhouse nurtures life

Bonfire flames warm
Marshmallow, chocolate, s'mores
Together with friends

Evening sun descends
Stars illuminate the sky
No sound but crickets

www.ingramcontent.com/pod-product-compliance
Lightning Source LLC
Chambersburg PA
CBHW040723060526
44119CB00083B/311